CW01086431

Horse Racing System Seeing The Light

My Other Books On Amazon

UK Professional Horse Racing Betting Edge Kindle Edition
https://www.amazon.co.uk/dp/B08JM3FV4M

Groupform UK Horse Racing System Kindle Edition
https://www.amazon.co.uk/dp/B084M4FSWN

The 6f 7f Furlong Hope Horse Lay System Simple To Use And Profitable Kindle Edition
https://www.amazon.co.uk/dp/B084RHCCSX

Horse Racing Betting Dutching System Kindle Edition
https://www.amazon.co.uk/dp/B08BDN5VGK

Betfair Place Market UK Horse Handicap System: Horse Racing Betting System Kindle Edition
https://www.amazon.co.uk/dp/B089FHPSM7

Introduction

Firstly many thanks for purchasing this UK horse racing system it is much appreciated and I think you might just see the light here!

This book is priced expensively for a reason! As you know I have written many books around UK handicap horse racing as these are the races I concentrate on. So what is so good about this horse racing system you may ask?

The system is so simple and easy to use and finds winners quickly! Most punters have busy lives and do not have time to trawl through horse form every day. I must stress that there will be days when the system picks no horses so please accept that and have a day off from betting.

Please note that all selections do not win!

In the book I have highlighted text in Red to emphasise important information you need to make sure you understand.

The horse racing system works on UK handicap races but you can apply it to UK non handicap races if you like. The book will cover mainly UK handicap races but I will put in a few non handicap race examples in here as well.

Please enjoy!

www.racingpost.com

www.betfair.com

www.chevanderwheil.com My personal website.

My Background

I graduated from University with a computer science degree many years ago when a degree meant something! I was always interested in horse racing and was fascinated in solving the UK horse racing form puzzle. I started my own computer business in my early 20's where I made good money and travelled across Europe. It was at this point in my life I decided to start a horse tipping business where I had weekly full page colour adverts in the Racing Post at £2K per advert and offices. I left the running of this horse tipping business to staff who were responsible for all parts of the business while I concentrated on my computer business.

In my late 30's around 1990 I decided to use my computer skills to computerise and model UK horse racing form using a database built with 10 years of detailed horse racing form. It was over a period of 2 years that I concentrated my efforts on UK handicap races in conjunction with the betting exchange Betfair. This is where I believed maximum profit could be gained.

The computer model allowed me to process 100's of handicap races per day and then formulate my system tweaking a horse's weight and BHB or OR (Official Rating). I must confess this was a difficult puzzle to crack even with a computer program written to crunch the data. I eventually found the correct weight and BHB rating for a horse based on its last performances in handicap races.

This book outlines this system and can be manually applied easily using the Racing Post on the internet.

Punter's can be fickle people where 95% of them could have no understanding of horse form and probability.

If you can back horses at higher prices then you will make money!

2

I regularly back horses that have a starting price of 2/1 and get 10/1!

Most punters want winners everyday regardless of the price and the horse's real chance of winning that race, this is where the bookmakers clean up.

Please take your time and practise this system and more importantly understand in-play betting odds on the Betfair exchange. You do not need to the use betting exchange you can back using normal bookmakers but make sure you get decent odds.

The Betfair Factor

Many punters use standard bookmakers but the better value is in-play betting on these selections on the Betfair exchange as you can see from the race examples in this book. When a race is in-play a horse's price will move erratically and sometimes spike out to 40.0 or 100.0!

So say a horse is 2/1 (3.0 Betfair) before the race starts you could ask for 10.0 in-play so you can see how much more profit you could make.

I can never understand why punters have not latched onto this!

What You Need To Get Started?

You will need access to the internet and the Racing Post website https://www.racingpost.com/

The Racing Post website is free and this is all that is required to use this horse racing system.

I use the Betfair betting exchange when placing my bets as I like to bet in-play.

https://www.betfair.com

How The System Works

The system works on 2 simple steps for UK races.

The 2 steps are as follows which I will go into with more detail later.

1. The horse must be the top BHB rated (OR - Official Rating) horse in the race. If more than one horse has the top rated you have to apply the system to all of these horses.
2. The difference between the horses current BHB rating (OR) and its rating (OR) for its second last race must be greater than or equal to 7 and less than 30.

You might think this is simple and yes it is and that's what we want!

There are too many pundits out there confusing punters I wonder why!

I only use this system in UK handicap horse races and it finds plenty of winners.

As mentioned previously you can use it for UK non-handicap races as well.

Food For Thought!

When I read the horse form I am one person analysing races and looking for an edge and the winner of a race. I suddenly realised the horse racing industry has 1000's of employed people inputting in some way or another to the race card and a horses BHB rating (OR) were analysts assess a horses past races. Now add the bookmaker into the equation and they price up a race and we know they are in the game to make money so they commit considerable resources at this as well.

So what am I getting at here?

A majority of the horse form and its ability has already been processed for you, i.e. the 1000's of people as mentioned before have helped you. Where punters go wrong is how they process and analyse this horse form data that is available to you free of charge!

This will become clearer when you start looking at the race examples in this book.

The Horse Racing System Explained

As previously mentioned you will need access to the racing post on the internet to use the system which is free.

https://www.racingpost.com/

Identify a UK handicap horse race you want to apply the horse racing system to and then follow the steps below.

We follow the 2 steps for an example race below.

19th October 2020 Windsor 2.30 Water's Edge 4/1 WON

So let's look into the 2 steps of the system in more detail below.

1. The horse must be the top BHB rating (OR - Official Rating) horse in the race. There can be more than one top rated horse in the race so we apply the system to these top rated horses.

If you look at a race card for a UK handicap and non handicap race each horse in that race will be allocated a BHB rating (OR – Official rating). This is a rating that the BHB has given to the horse based on its past runs in races. The higher the OR the better the horse is. So if we look at the race card below for the 19th October 2020 Windsor 2.30 I have highlighted in blue the top OR rated horses which have an OR 80.

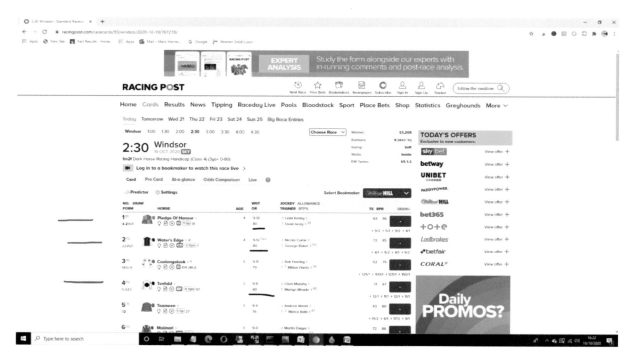

So horses Pledge Of Honour, Water's Edge and Tenfold have a OR 80 as underlined in black on the race card. So we have 3 top rated horses in this race to consider normally you would get 1 top rated horse but you apply the system to all top rated horses.

This race is a handicap as denoted in the title of the race next to the time of the race. You can apply this system to non handicap horse races as well.

So step 1 is quite easy just take note of the top OR rated horses on the race card using the racing post on the internet which is free.

Let's move on to step 2.

2. The difference between the horses current BHB rating and its rating for its second last race must be greater than or equal to 7 and less than 30.

This is the important step and you might think how strange but there is a reason for this.

I mentioned earlier there are 1000's of people involved in horse racing and assessing a horse's form and the ability to win a race is part of it. I also mentioned that a horses BHB rating or OR is allocated to a horse based on its past races. This OR rating is constantly evaluated by horse racing bodies to ensure they can allocate the correct weight in handicap races.

A horses BHB rating (OR) can go up and can go down, most go down as a horse gets older i.e. the horse will hit a maximum OR and then start to decline unless they are Group horses which tend to get retired to stud before they decline.

In step 2 we are trying to determine if a horse in a race is improving i.e. it's BHB rating (OR) is increasing. We can check this by looking at the 2nd last race the horse ran in and obtaining the OR the horse ran off and comparing it to the OR on the race card it's running off today (the race we are analysing for a possible bet).

By using the horses 2nd last race and not the last race we determine if the horse has improved over its last two races and this is confirmed by OR the horse is running off in the race card.

So if we take the horse Water's Edge on the race card above it has an OR 80 as indicated in black on the race card. Now let's look at its 2nd last race the horse ran in which we can check by clicking on the horses name in the race card.

If you look at the screen shot below for the horse Water's Edge you can see the horses 2nd last race was on the 13th September 2020 with OR 73 underlined in black. We do not use the horse's last race on the 12th October 2020 OR 75.

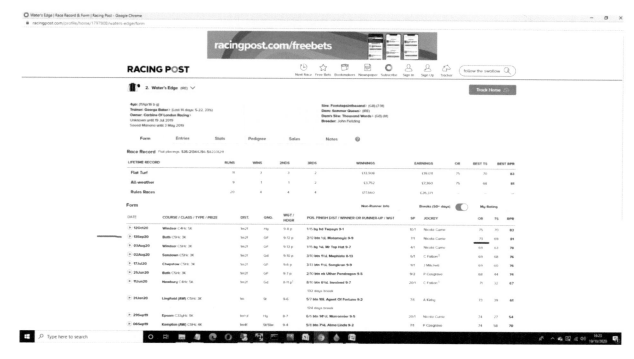

So we can see the horse has improved from 73 to 75 and to 80.

We now subtract the 2nd last race OR which is 73 from the OR 80 the on the race card i.e. the race we are analysing for a bet 80-73=+7

BHB DIFF +7

This horse passes step 2 as the BHB DIFF must be greater than or equal to 7 and less than 30.

This horse did go on to win the race at 4/1 much higher on Betfair!

Recap of step 2 below,

'Step 2 The difference between the horses current BHB rating and its rating for its second last race must be greater than or equal to 7 and less than 30.'

By using the 2nd last race you have more form data to determine if a horse has improved enough to warrant a bet.

Now how did I get to the magic values of 7 and 30 range for the BHB DIFF variable?

By analysing 100's and 100's of past races on my own database it's as simple as that!

Now let's not forget about the other two top rated horses on the race card Pledge Of Honour and Tenfold and why they were not selected i.e. they did not pass step 2.

We click on the horse Pledge Of Honour on the race card

Pledge Of Honour 2nd last race was on the 17th August 2020 OR 75 and we know it's running off an OR 80 in today's race card so 80-75=+5

BHB DIFF +5

As it is +5 it does not pass step 2.

Note: Pledge Of Honour last race on the 18th September, 2020 OR was also 75 which indicates the horse has not really improved between its 2nd last race and its last race.

Now let's look at the other top rated horse we click on the horse Tenfold on the race card

Tenfold 2nd last race was the 29th June 2020 OR 77 and we know it OR 80 on the race card today so this gives us 80-77=+3

BHB DIFF +3

So this horse did not pass step 2 has BHB DIFF is less than 7.

Note: Again the horse Tenfold had not really improved in its last 2 races!

So if we look at the result of the race below, Water's Edge won the race and Pledge Of Honour finished 8th and Tenfold finished 9th.

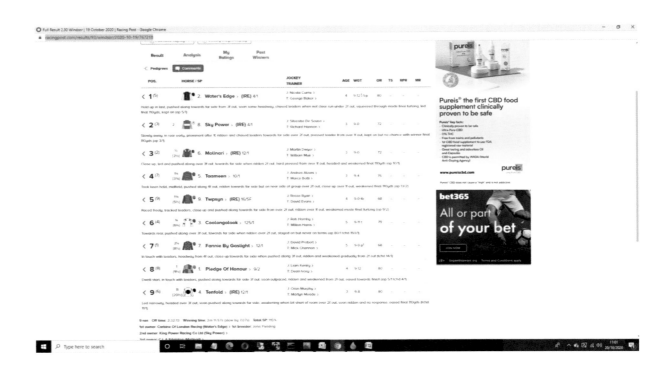

This system is easy to apply and quick we are basically using the official BHB rating (OR) that has been assessed by many people and identifying improving horses based on the horses current OR mark on the race card and it's 2nd last race OR mark.

Make sure you understand this system before moving on to the detailed example races.

Final Comment About Horse Selection Odds

If you find a horse that passes the 2 steps in the horse racing system look at what price is being offered on the exchanges like https://www.betfair.com and bookmaker prices on https://www.oddschecker.com if the horses is 50/1 then would you really back this horse?

I mentioned earlier bookmakers commit a great deal of effort in pricing up a horse in a race. Yes some do win at large odds. I like horses that are in the top 3 odds in the betting market thus using the bookmaker's and exchange knowledge in conjunction with this horse racing system. To get the edge!

Detailed Example Races

In the detailed examples I show the result of the race to get the top OR of the race it is the same OR as would be on the race card on the days racing.

17th October 2020 Wolverhampton 4.55 Rogue Tide Won 6/1

BHB DIFF +8

We know it's a handicap race by looking at the race title near the time of the race and you can see the word 'handicap' in the race title.

Please see screenshot below.

In this race on the 17th October 2020 the horse Rogue Tide had a BHB rating (OR) of 68 which I have highlighted in red above. This is the OR rating you will see when you look at the race card for the race in the racing post on the days racing. The horse must have the highest OR rating on the race card!

So we are looking at the horse with the highest OR on the race card and this is the key to this system!

Now let's look at the method behind this race.

We know the race was run on the 17th October 2020 I have marked in blue above where Rogue Tide had a BHB Rating (OR) of 68 marked in grey which I have previously mentioned above. This makes the horse's second last race 23rd September 2020 marked in red and had an OR of 60 marked in black. We are not interested in its last race on the 7th October 2020, this system works on the horses 2nd last race and that is very important!!!!

So we simply subtract the last race 23rd September 2020 OR 60 from the OR of the race the horse is running in i.e. today's race on the 17th October 2020 which is 68.

So 68-60 = +8

BHB DIFF +8

So this meets our criteria of selecting horses where OR difference has to be greater than or equal to 7 and less than 30. This shows how simple this system is and this was a nice winner on the day.

16th October 2020 Haydock 3.48 Trumpet Man Won 11/4

BHB DIFF +14

This horse had been improving considerably in its last races!

The horse had the highest OR on the race card of 86 highlighted in red below. Once again we are only interested in horses with the highest OR for the race.

In the screenshot above the horse Trumpet Man was running off a BHB rating of 86 (OR) highlighted in red above.

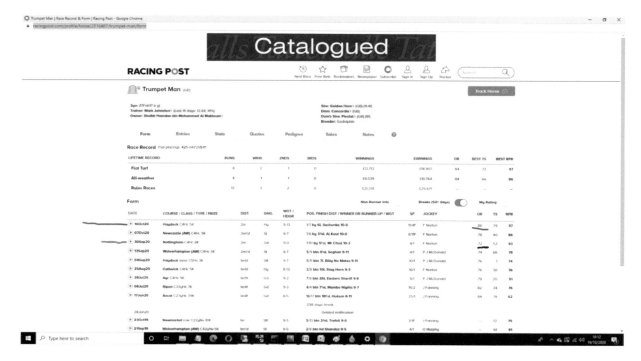

We know the race was run on the 16th October 2020 I have marked in blue above where it had a BHB Rating (OR) of 86 marked in grey which I have previously mentioned above. This makes the horse's second last race 30rd September 2020 marked in red and had an OR of 72 marked in black.

So we simply subtract the 2nd last race 30th September 2020 OR 72 from the OR of the race the horse is running in i.e. today's race on the 16th October 2020 which is 86.

So 86-72 = +14

BHB DIFF +14

So this meets our criteria of selecting horses where OR difference has to be greater than or equal to 7 and less than 30. This shows how simple this system is and another winner on the day.

8th October 2020 Exeter 1.30 Espalion Won 9/2

BHB DIFF +10

This was another horse that was improving fast and has the highest OR 119 on the race card that day.

In the screenshot above the horse Espalion was running off a BHB rating of 119 (OR) highlighted in red above.

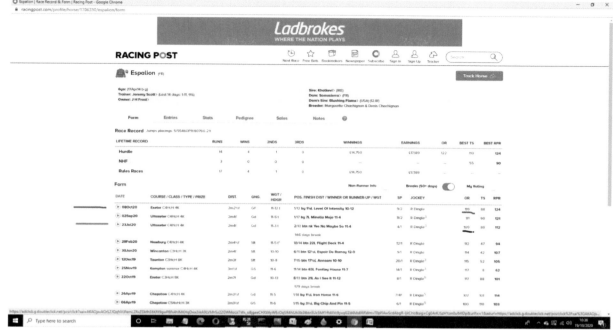

We know the race was run on the 8th October 2020 I have marked in blue above where it had a BHB Rating (OR) of 119 marked in grey. This makes the horse's second last race 23rd July 2020 marked in red and had an OR of 109 marked in black.

So we simply subtract the 2nd last race 23rd July 2020 OR 109 from the OR of the race the horse is running in i.e. today's race on the 8th October 2020 which is 119.

So 119-109 = +10

BHB DIFF +10

So this meets our criteria of selecting horses where OR difference has to be greater than or equal to 7 and less than 30. This shows how simple this system is and another winner on the day.

I like the 9/2 price but more profit can be made in-running on Betfair!

7th October 2020 Nottingham 3.10 Snow Ocean 2nd 7/2

BHB DIFF +9

It is important to show an example of horses that have not won as we know all horses do not win!

There were two horses with the highest OR 85 on the race card for the 7th October 2020 which where Eagle Court and Snow Ocean so we would look at both of these horses in turn and apply the horse racing system.

See screen shot below.

The horse Eagle Court did qualify for Step 1 of the system but did not pass step 2 as the BHB DIFF value was +3. Eagle Court 2nd last race was on the 15th September 2020 with OR 82 so 85-82=+3 proving it did not pass step 2 of the horse racing system.

We can see the horse Snow Ocean marked in blue above came 2nd on the 7th October 2020 with a OR 85 highlighted in red above.

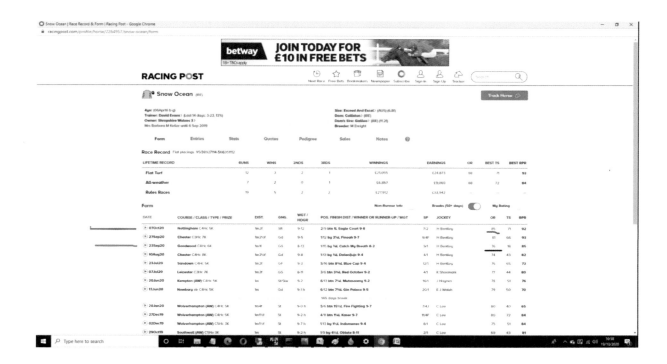

By now you should understand how this simple system works.

After performing our OR subtraction 85-76 gives us a BHB DIFF +9 so this horse qualified.

This system will find winners on a regular basis but we have to accept losers, but do we?

If you use betting exchanges like Betfair you can perform a back to lay on your selection to minimise your risk and even better green the field so which ever horse wins the race you make money!

The horse Eagle Court did win the race at 6/1 and Snow Ocean was 2nd

6th October 2020 Lingfield 4.10 Miaella Won 9/4F

BHB DIFF +17

This was a large BHB DIFF value of +17 and duly won the race.

There were 4 horses with a top OR 65 Miaella, Lordsbridge Boy, Princely, Giovanni Tiepolo and this was a tight handicap race indeed. Only the horse Miaella qualified for this race as the other 3 horses did not pass the second step of this system.

Lordsbridge Boy   BHB DIFF +3 2nd last race date 3rd September 2020 OR 62

Princely BHB DIFF +3   2nd last race date 6th August 2020 OR 62

Giovanni Tiepolo BHB DIFF -3   2nd last race date 2nd August 2020 OR 68

The horse Miaella ran the race on the 6th October 2020 ran with a OR rating 65 marked in red above.

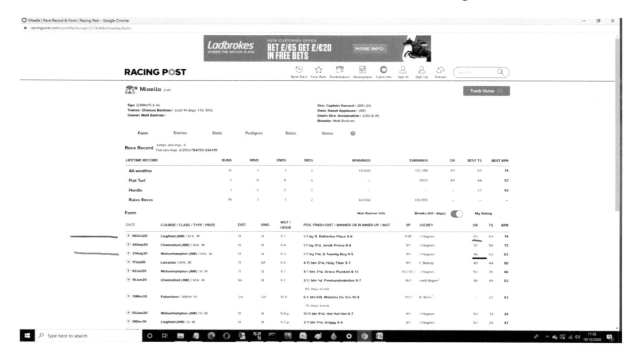

The horse Miaella ran it's race on the 6th October 2020 with a OR 65 and ran its 2nd last race on the 21st August 2020 running with a OR 48.

So doing our OR subtraction 65-48= +17

BHB DIFF +17

The horse Miaella had improved significantly between its 2nd last race and last race and then the current OR rating was increased again for the race on the 6th October 2020!

2nd October 2020 Fontwell 3.20 Pres Won 11/4

BHB DIFF +10

There was carnage in the race with many horses pulling up and unseating. There were 3 top rated OR 117 horses in this race Pres, Buster Edwards and One Of Us. Only horse Pres passed step 2 of the system with a BHB DIFF +10 the other two horses did qualify for step 2.

Buster Edwards BHB DIFF +1   2nd last race date 7th March 2020 OR 116

One Of Us BHB DIFF -3 2nd last race date 30th January 2020 OR 120

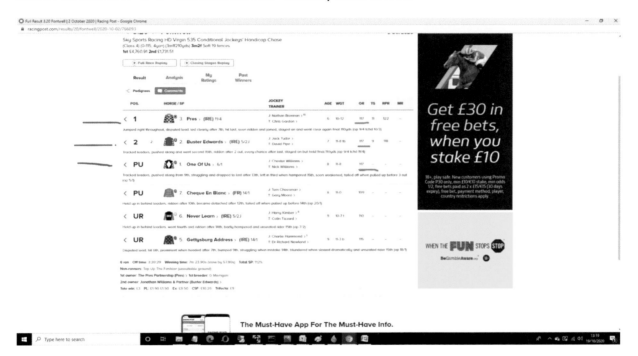

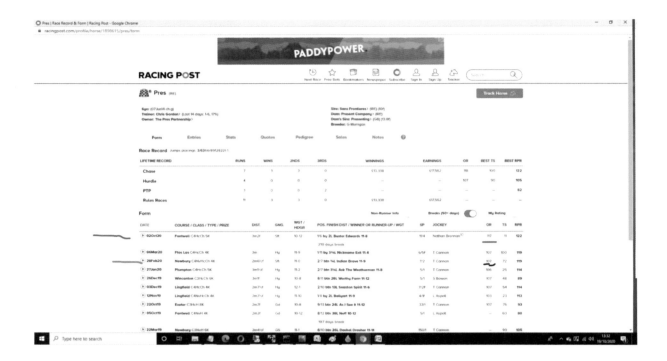

Horse Pres was running off an OR 117 on the race on the 2nd October 2020 marked in blue and its 2nd last race was on the 28th February, 2020 with an OR 107 marked in red. This horse passed step 2 with BHB DIFF +10

The horse had not improved between its 2nd last race and last race but still had a hefty BHB DIFF +10 value!

2nd October 2020 Ascot 3.05 Raaeq Won 13/8F

BHB DIFF +8

This was an easy winner by 5 lengths not my type of price though but a winner is a winner!

Raaeq was the top rated OR 97 in the race on the 2nd October 2020 and passed steps 1 and 2 of the system.

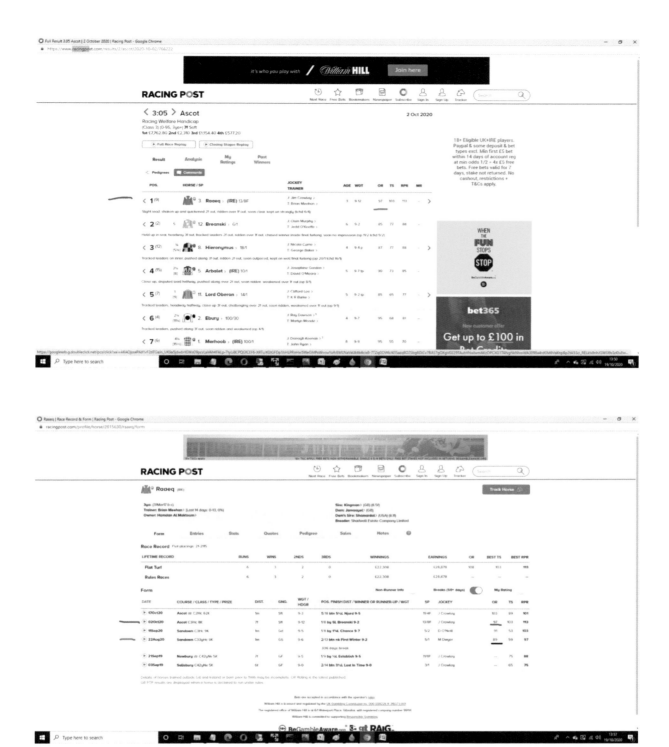

Raaeq ran in the race on the 2nd October 2020 with OR 97 as highlighted in blue in the above screenshot. Its 2nd last race on the 22nd August 2020 it ran with a OR 89 as highlighted in red.

Using our BHB DIFF calculation 97-89= +8

BHB DIFF +8

This horse did not trade very high in-play on Betfair only reached decimal odds 2.86

19

1st September 2020 Ripon 1.00 Winter Power Won 6/5F   (Non Handicap Race)

BHB DIFF +7

I wanted to show an example of a UK non-handicap race this was a bit short priced for me I tend to stay to handicap races but punters have a choice.

Winter power was clear on OR of 89 with next best Risk Of Thunder OR 82

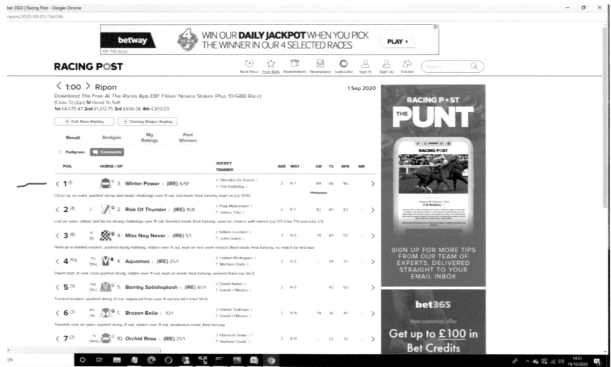

Winter Power 2nd last race was on the 30th July 2020 OR 82 giving it a BHB DIFF 89-82=+7

See screen shot below.

The horse passes both steps of the horse racing system.

So we apply the horse racing system in the same way to UK handicap and non handicap races!

BHB DIFF +7

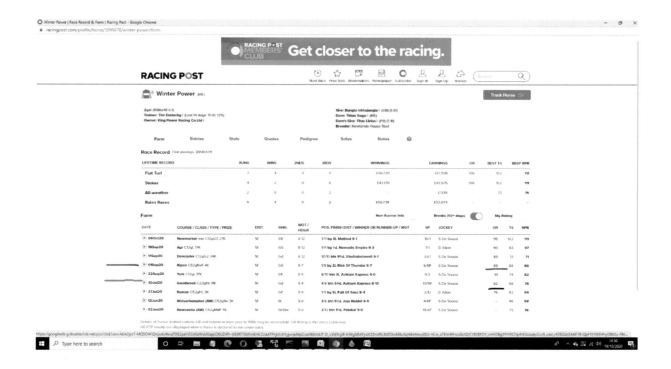

5th September 2020 Stratford 2.25 For Pleasure Won 9/4   (Non Handicap Race)

BHB DIFF +17

This horse had a high BHB DIFF value and was obviously on the improve. The horse was running off an OR 124 on the 5th September 2020 and was the highest in the race. It's 2nd last race on the 21st July 2020 OR 107. So our BHB DIFF value calculated 124-107=+17.

See screen shot below.

As a side note on the 18th October 2020 the horse ran in a race where it was stepped up in class and ran off an OR 144 and came 4th beaten a long way. The horse was improving up to that point but maybe it's now hit its ceiling or it was stepping up in class too quickly.

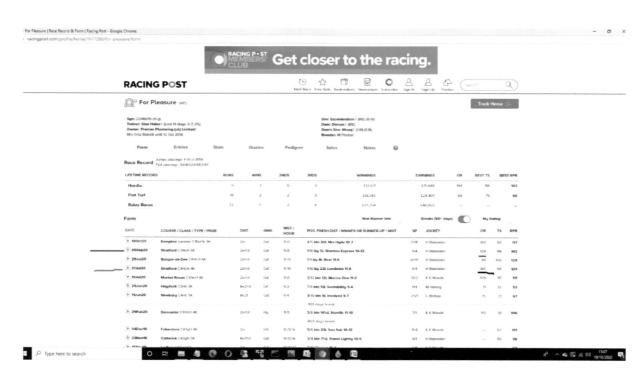

Condensed Examples July-September 2020 UK Races

1st July 2020   Southwell 12:00 Nineohtwooneoh 2/1F Won   BHB DIFF +10

3rd July 2020 Chepstow 2:50 Queen Of Silca 2/1F Won BHB DIFF +9

4th July 2020 Haydock 4:25 It's Good To Laugh 8/1 2nd BHB DIFF +7   (Horse was beaten by a nose!)

7th July 2020 Leicester 7:13 Win O'Clock 11/10F Won BHB DIFF +9

7th July 2020 Stratford 12:15 Dagueneau 1/2F Won BHB DIFF +11   (Non Handicap Race)

9th July 2020 Newmarket 1:50 Al Suhail 5/2 Won BHB DIFF +7 (Non Handicap Race)

10th July 2020 Bath 7:35 Songkran 9/2 Won BHB DIFF +7

2nd August 2020 Sandown 12:00 Seneca Chief 9/1 Won BHB DIFF +11

4th August 2020 Lingfield 6:15 Cappananty Con 8/1 Won BHB DIFF +12

5th August 2020 Newton Abbot 3:20 Pagero 5/4 Won BHB DIFF +15

5th August 2020 Newton Abbot 3:50 Soldier Of Love Won Evens BHB DIFF +11

8th August 2020 Uttoxeter 6:30 The Boola Bee Won 6/1 BHB DIFF +11

8th August 2020 Haydock 4:25 Aristocratic Lady Won Evens BHB DIFF +13

9th August 2020 Salisbury 4:30 Awesomedude Won 6/4 BHB DIFF +13

1st September 2020 Hamilton 7:45 Kayewhykelly 6/4 Won BHB DIFF +10

1st September 2020 Ripon 1:00 Winter Power 6/5 Won BHB DIFF +7 (Non Handicap Race)

5th September 2020 Stratford 5:20 Tikkinthebox 5/1 Won BHB DIFF +7

5th September 2020 Ascot 3:05 Cepheus 16/1 2nd BHB DIFF +10

5th September 2020 Stratford 2:25 For Pleasure 9/4 Won BHB DIFF +17 (Non Handicap Race)

I back my horses on the Betfair exchange and ask for higher prices in-play sometimes 10.0 for a horse whose starting price is decimal 3.0!

Final Comment

I hope you enjoyed the book and will enjoy betting on horses even more.

Horse racing is very hard indeed and not many people succeed that's why bookmakers exist!

I have mentioned several times taking in-play prices on Betfair for better value this is how you really make bigger profits in the long run backing horses at higher prices than their current price before the race goes in-play.

What amazes me is how punters cannot read basic horse form or they are too lazy and like throwing their money away, we live in a crazy world.

If you need any support email me at

vanderwheil6@gmail.com

My Personal Website

https://chevanderwheil.com

Happy Punting!

Printed in Great Britain
by Amazon